SCIENCE FAIR
HOW TO DO A SUCCESSFUL PROJECT

EARTH SCIENCE

BY
SHIRLEY COX

SERIES CONSULTANT
DR. JOHN M. LAMMERT
Associate Professor of Biology
Gustavus Adolphus College
St. Peter, Minnesota

**ROURKE
PUBLICATIONS
INC.**
Vero Beach, FL 32964
U.S.A.

LIBRARY OF CONGRESS CATALOGUING-IN-PUBLICATION DATA

Cox, Shirley 1953–
   Earth science / by Shirley Cox
      p. cm. — (Science fair)
   Summary: Explains the scientific method and suggests a variety of earth
science projects and experiments suitable for a science fair.
   ISBN 0-86625-429-3
   1. Earth sciences—Experiments—Juvenile literature. 2. Science projects—
Juvenile literature. [1. Earth sciences—Experiments. 2. Experiments.
3. Science projects.] I. Title II. Series.
QE44.C68 1992
550' .78—dc20
                                                  92-9132
                                                            CIP
                                                             AC

DESIGNED & PRODUCED BY:
MARK E. AHLSTROM
(The Bookworks)

PHOTOGRAPHY:
Cover–THE IMAGE BANK/Yves Lefeure
Text–MARK E. AHLSTROM

The publisher and author accept no responsibility for any harm that
may occur as a result of using information contained in this book.

TABLE OF CONTENTS

CHAPTER 1. *What Makes a Science Project "Scientific?"* 4

CHAPTER 2. *Choosing Plants As A Topic For Your Project* 10
Types of Projects 10
Testing with Controlled Experiments 12
Testing with Predictions 14
Stating Your Purpose 18

CHAPTER 3. *Planning Your Project* 21
More About Experimental Design 21
Lab Notebook 22
Time Schedule 25

CHAPTER 4. *Doing Your Project* 26
Safety 26
Keeping A Record of Your Results 27
Analyzing Results 30
Drawing Conclusions 32

CHAPTER 5. *Presenting Your Project* 33
Writing A Report 33
Making Graphs to Show Your Data 35
Organizing Your Display 38
Talking to the Judges or to Your Class 41
Judging of Your Project 42
Final Words of Encouragement 44

SUPPLIES 45

GLOSSARY 46

INDEX 48

CHAPTER 1

What Makes a Science Project "Scientific?"

How do you feel about doing a science fair project? If you decided to do one yourself, you are probably very excited. If your teacher has assigned a project as a class requirement, you may not feel quite so happy about it. You may even be feeling a little afraid. Once you understand how to use the **scientific method**, your fear should disappear. It will be replaced with the excitement of doing something challenging and fun. Why should this miracle occur? Because there are no wrong ideas, wrong experiments, or wrong <u>observations</u>! In fact, you can't be wrong. You can start with any idea. The scientific method will help you choose a reasonable idea. If you make errors, you don't even have to know it! The scientific method will help you pinpoint mistakes and help you decide what changes to make.

When you're using the scientific method, even the "wrong" results can be "good" results. Take the example of Dr. Spencer Silver.

Dr. Silver worked in product development at the 3M company. Many years ago he had the problem of developing a strong, permanent glue. Using the scientific method, he planned and conducted an experiment. When Dr. Silver tested the product that was formed, he found that it wasn't a strong glue at all. It was barely sticky and not at all permanent. The experiment was a failure and Dr. Silver had to try again.

Several years later, another scientist at the 3M company, Art Fry, was upset. He was always losing his notes and page markers in a book he was using. Then he thought of Dr. Silver's experiment. Mr. Fry used the barely-sticky glue to create the product sold today as self-stick notes!

Self-stick notes prove there are no "wrong" answers.

So what is this scientific method?

The scientific method is a way to answer questions and solve problems. It involves a series of steps that are followed in a logical order. Scientists use it to find explanations for things they have observed. When scientists notice something new or interesting, they wonder "What is that? Why did that happen?" A problem has been identified. Now the scientist will form a **hypothesis** to explain the observation. A hypothesis is a possible answer that is based on knowledge about the problem. This knowledge comes from finding out what other scientists have already learned about similar problems.

Not all scientists agree on the order of the steps when using the scientific method. Different problems often require a different order. However, scientists do agree on what the necessary steps are. A typical sequence is shown in the chart below.

Steps Followed in the Scientific Method

✔ Make an observation.

✔ State the problem: What do you want to find out?

✔ What is already known about the observation?

✔ Develop a hypothesis: What do you think is a reasonable explanation for the observation?

✔ Design an experiment that will provide answers: What materials will be needed and how will they be used.

✔ Record data or observations: What happened during the experiment?

✔ Analyze the results.

✔ Draw a conclusion: Did your data support your hypothesis? What did you learn? What do your results mean?

As long as all the steps are included and followed in a logical order, the scientific method will work for you.

Now let's look at an example of an observation and a hypothesis. Look at the picture of tombstones in a cemetery. What observations tell you that a grave marker is old? You might check for rounded edges, smoothed designs, or blurry letters. New markers have sharp edges. You probably know that the action of wind and rain over time causes the **weathering** of rocks. Have you also heard of acid rain? As the problem of air pollution has increased, rain has become more acidic. Gases from pollutants react with water in the air to form acid. What will acid rain do to the markers in the cemetery? One hypothesis might be "Acid rain will speed up the weathering of rocks."

Weathering makes this tombstone look old.

Next, a scientist makes a plan to test the hypothesis. This plan is the **experimental design**. Before any work can start, materials must be chosen and a plan for their use in the experiment must be written. The experimenter must also decide what observations and measurements need to be made.

To test our hypothesis about the action of acid rain on rocks, we could use the following plan.

Marble, a rock commonly used in buildings and monuments, will be placed in two groups of plastic jars. Five jars will have tap water, and five jars will have vinegar, an acid, added to the water. Each jar will contain one marble chip. The group of jars with marble chips in tap water are called the **control**. They will show what changes are due to water alone, since no acid is added to the water. When the jars have been prepared, the experiment can begin.

Be sure to label the groups in an experiment.

During the experiment **data** are collected. This means that what is seen and measured is recorded. In our example, we must make observations that will let us compare changes to the marble chips in the two groups of jars. **Mass** is a measure of the amount of matter present. Since weathering removes small particles of rock, the mass of a large rock may decrease as it weathers. We could measure the mass of each marble chip every day for two weeks. We could also record observations about the appearance of the liquid and the shapes of the marble chips. If our hypothesis is right, the marble chips in acid water should lose more mass that those in tap water.

Next the results are studied. What happened to the mass of each marble chip? How do the shapes of the chips kept in acid compare to those in tap water? What happened to the liquid in the jars? Were there any unexpected changes?

Finally, from these results, conclusions are made. Was the hypothesis correct? If not, what would be another hypothesis? Should the experiment be redesigned or repeated before the hypothesis is accepted or rejected?

The data produced in one experiment, or even a series of experiments, often lead to new questions and more experiments. Even the work of a Nobel Prize-winning scientist produces more questions than answers. These questions are often worth further investigation.

Scientists know that their work is never done.

CHAPTER 2

Choosing Earth Science as a Topic for Your Project

What makes a successful science project? The hardest part is selecting a topic. Spending some time to think about a number of ideas will help insure the success of your final choice. The best topics will be those that interest you. You will be excited to design and try out these experiments. Your science project will no longer be a task assigned by your teacher, but your own creative idea. Your idea doesn't have to be complex or hard to do, especially if this is your first project. Great projects often focus on something simple.

Earth scientists study the weather, rocks, oceans, and the sky. This book will guide you through the basic steps you need to follow in order to do a good earth science project. You will not find step-by-step instructions. Instead, you will discover ways to use your own imagination and creative powers. Projects that you create will be fun to do!

What types of projects can you do about earth science?

If you could visit a science fair to look at the projects, you would probably see three different types:

★ *Exhibits* display collections or explain a topic.
★ *Demonstrations* repeat an experiment found in a book.
★ *Investigations* use the scientific method to solve a problem.

Because of the way the projects are judged, the first two types often receive lower scores and fewer awards. They are less scientific than an

10

investigation. You may wish to find out how your project will be judged. There may be restrictions on the type of project you can do. Perhaps your teacher can review your plan and help you find out if it meets the fair's rules.

If all your ideas seem to be exhibits or demonstrations, don't panic. The next part of this book will help you understand some of the ways earth scientists investigate problems. Think about the examples. Then use them to help you change your simple idea into a winning project!

☞ *Exhibits*

Exhibits can be good science projects if they are creative and done well. Like a **geologist**, you could collect and classify rocks. You could display a fossil collection and explain how fossils are dated. You could make a very interesting exhibit that tells how gems like diamonds and rubies are formed.

Like an **oceanographer**, you could build a model showing the mountains, ridges, and trenches of the Atlantic Ocean. The animals that inhabit different areas of the oceans—dark depths, coral reefs, rocky shores, and sandy beaches—could make a colorful exhibit. An exhibit could be made that shows ocean currents and waves, including the Gulf Stream and **tsunamis**.

A **meteorology** exhibit could tell about several kinds of storms— tornadoes, hurricanes, thunderstorms, and blizzards. A collection of weather instruments, and a description of how each is used, could become an exhibit.

An **astronomy** exhibit could show the constellations. You could also make a telescope and explain in your exhibit how it works.

☞ *Demonstrations*

Demonstrations show how things happen and help us understand why. The layering, folding, and faulting of the earth's surface are topics in geology that can be demonstrated using layers of colored clay. A fan can produce a wind over water to show how waves form or over a pile of sand to show how dunes are made. A Faucault pendulum can be made to demonstrate the earth's rotation.

Making an exhibit or doing a demonstration may not get you the first-place ribbon. However, learning about an earth science problem and collecting samples of things is often the start of an earth scientist's work. If you are ready to do more and to learn more, you might want to turn an exhibit or demonstration into something more. The next section will give you some ideas.

☞ *Investigations*

The science fair projects that earn the highest awards are usually investigations. Investigations use the scientific method to answer a question. Whenever possible, scientists prefer to test a hypothesis by doing an experiment. Conclusions drawn from an experiment are based on facts that can be rechecked at any time.

Testing with Controlled Experiments

An experiment is used to discover how changing one **variable** affects another. Any condition that changes during an experiment is called a variable. One variable is changed on purpose by the scientist. It is called the **independent variable**. The scientist watches for changes in a second variable called the **dependent variable**.

What are the variables in our acid rain experiment? The water in one group of jars was made more acidic on purpose to represent acid rain. Acidity is the independent variable. What do we expect to change as a result of acid rain? We decided the mass of the marble chip might change. This mass is the dependent variable.

In planning an experiment, scientists decide how they want to change the independent variable and how to measure the change in the dependent variable. They try to think of other possible variables that might affect the results. Because they try to control these other variables, the experiment is called a controlled experiment.

In our acid rain experiment, there are two groups of jars. They differ in only one way—only one group contains acid. The jars containing acid are the **experimental group**. The jars containing water without acid are the **control group**. What other variables must be controlled? Each jar must be the same size, contain the same amount of liquid, and the same number of marble chips. Each one must be shaken the same amount and allowed to sit on a shelf for the same length of time. When the experiment is finished, we will be able to compare the two groups of jars. Any differences will only be due to the acid in the experimental group.

Thinking about the variables you can change and observe in an experiment will help you develop an idea for an earth science investigation. Thinking about how the experimental group will compare to the control group will help you write a hypothesis.

The chart below shows several problems for which the independent and dependent variable have been listed. The last column contains a hypothesis. One way to begin a science fair project is to make a chart like this for the problems you might want to investigate.

Possible Earth Science Investigations

PROBLEM	INDEPENDENT VARIABLE	DEPENDENT VARIABLE	HYPOTHESIS
Effect of pebble shape on movement by water	Shape of pebbles: flat, round, angular	Distance pebble is moved down a trough by flowing water	Flatter pebbles will move least since water will pass over them.
Effect of wind speed on drying of soil	Speed of fan: fast, medium, slow	Time needed to dry out a soil sample	The faster the fan blows across the soil, the faster it will dry out.
Effect of dissolved salt on evaporation rate	Amount of salt dissolved in water	Time needed for water to evaporate	Salt slows down evaporation.
Effect of soil type on plant growth	Type of crushed rock: limestone, basalt, granite	Height of bean plants	Bean plants will grow taller in soil that comes from limestone.
Effect of launching angle on distance a projectile travels	Angle of launch	Distance projectile travels	Projectiles launched with the lowest angle will travel the least distance.

The following list contains some other problems which could be investigated using controlled experiments:

★ What materials are good insulators?
★ Does sterilizing soil have an effect on the growth of plants?
★ Does crystal size depend on the temperature of the solution?
★ Does the shape of a crystal depend on the shape of the dish it is growing in?
★ What is the best amount of fertilizer to add to soil?
★ How does salt water affect fish?
★ Are the effects of humidity different on hair from different animals?
★ Do hot and cold water evaporate at the same rate?
★ How do different materials compare in reflecting light?
★ What happens to the brightness of a light as distance is increased?

Testing with Predictions

Many of the questions that interest earth scientists cannot be investigated by doing controlled experiments. For example, a geologist might think that ice in the center of a glacier flows faster than the ice at its edges. However, a scientist can't design a controlled experiment with a glacier because many variables (such as thickness, pressure, and composition) cannot be controlled. The earth scientist must use some other method to test this kind of hypothesis.

A good hypothesis leads to a **prediction**. If a prediction turns out to be correct, then it supports this hypothesis. For example, the geologist interested in glaciers might predict that a straight row of stakes across a glacier will become curved over time if the center of the glacier moves faster than its edges. The geologist could visit a glacier, drive in the row of stakes, and wait to see what happens.

The chart on the next page lists several hypotheses that cannot be tested by a controlled experiment. Next to each hypothesis is a prediction that could be checked.

Testing Predictions

HYPOTHESIS	PREDICTIONS
Temperature changes determine the rate of glacial movement.	Glaciers move faster in summer than in winter.
Air pressure decreases with altitude.	A barometer will read less on top of a tall building than on the ground floor.
A west wind brings rain.	When it's raining, the wind is from the west, never the north, south, or east.
Kentucky was once under the ocean.	Limestone in Kentucky contains fossil coral and sea shells.
Sunspots are tides on the sun produced by the gravity of the inner planets.	More sunspots can be seen when Mercury, Venus, and Earth are in a line than when they are not.

☞ Field Studies

Field studies are one way earth scientists check predictions. The geologist interested in glaciers would be doing a field study by placing and observing rows of stakes in glaciers. A field study requires careful observations and measurements that are made "in the field," out in nature where the events are happening. If you like outdoor activities, you may want to plan a field study for your project. The following is a list of problems that could be investigated with a field study. Use these ideas to help you think of your own field studies:

★ Does creep of soil down a hillside make trees slant?
★ What is the rate of movement of rock on a **talus** slope?
★ What do exposed layers of rock reveal about the past history of the area?
★ What produces acidic or basic environments in nature?
★ Do different environments differ in the pH of soil and water?
★ What shapes a shoreline?
★ How does the ecology of a lagoon compare to that of an open shore?
★ What microclimates exist in a cave?
★ How much does the temperature vary in an animal's burrow?

Even young earth scientists get to spend time "in the field."

☞ Models

Earth scientists can also check their predictions by making a model. Models are built so that they behave like the real thing. An oceanographer may not have the time or money to study the movement of ocean water between the earth's equator and its poles. The effect of temperature on the movement of water can be studied in a model ocean—a tank full of water that is cooled at one end and heated at the other. A **paleontologist** might think that certain marks on a fossil bone were made by a stone knife. The scientist could imitate the action of a stone on real bone to see if similar marks are made.

A stream table is a favorite model used by geologists. It can be set up to act like a real river in order to study the effect of variables like water speed, bank erosion, and the shape of the river valley. A ripple tank is another model system. It is used to study the action of waves in water.

Perhaps you are interested in a problem that involves a feature not located close enough for you to do a field study. If so, you might think of how you could build a model to test your hypothesis. Your school or a local college might have a stream table or a ripple tank that you could use. If not, you might be able to build one yourself.

The following chart lists some problems and suggests a model that might be useful in studying the problem.

Using Models

PROBLEM	MODEL
What is the relationship between water speed and stream width?	stream table
How does a delta form?	stream table
How does the movement of a glacier affect various bedding materials?	ice on a stream table
What is the relationship between slope and stream formation?	stream table
Could a single layer of fossil shells have been deposited at different times originally in different layers of sediment?	stream table
How is sonar or radar used to measure distance?	ball bouncing off a wall
What do the patterns traced by a seismograph mean about the motions in the earth's crust?	shaking a table
What kinds of faults are produced when rock layers push together or pull apart?	sand layers in a clear box with a moveable wall
Do waves cause the mixing of surface and deep water in a lake?	aquarium of water and a fan
Does water in a wave move differently in shallow and deep water?	ripple tank
How do waves behave when they reach a beach or a barrier?	ripple tank
How does the rate of cooling affect the size and shape of crystals in igneous rock?	melted moth flakes
What happens to rock crystals when high pressure forms metamorphic rock?	moth flakes squeezed in a vise

Stating Your Purpose

Once you have selected the earth science problem you want to study, you are ready to write a clear statement of its purpose. For our acid rain experiment, here are two choices:

> The purpose of this project is to determine if acid rain increases the rate of weathering of marble.
> Does the rate of weathering increase when marble is exposed to acid rain?

Each of these sentences states the purpose clearly, and also makes a prediction about the results. If the statement explains the problem clearly, it will also indicate the measurements that will be made and the data that will be collected.

Soon you will be ready to begin your lab notebook. Stating the purpose of the investigation will be one of the first entries. A more detailed explanation of the lab notebook can be found in Chapter 3.

Gathering Information for Your Project

Your search for information should begin in a library. This is where you will find books, encyclopedias, magazines and newspapers that contain articles about earth science. You will also find librarians ready to help you find things about your topic. Be sure to ask for their help.

You can use the card catalog or on-line computer catalog to find out what books the library has. In the subject catalog, look under the headings "Earth Science," "Science Experiments," or other key words suggested by the ideas you are considering. If you have trouble, the librarian can help you.

The Reader's Guide to Periodical Literature will help you find magazines that contain articles about earth science. Use the subject headings again to find a list of articles. Each entry will show the name and volume of the magazine, as well as the title and page numbers of the article. If there are articles you want to read, you will probably have to ask the librarian to get the magazines for you.

*The Reader's Guide to Periodical Literature will help you
find magazine articles.*

Since you can't expect to remember everything you read, you will need to make some notes while you are at the library. Write your notes on 3" x 5" index cards. Later, you can select the most useful cards and arrange them in the best order. Each card should contain notes from only one source. For magazines write down the name of the author, the title of the article, the name of the magazine, the volume number, and the date. For books, write down the title, author's name, publisher, and the date and place of publication. As you read, record the page numbers and write your notes.

If you copy exact words, mark this section of your notes by enclosing it in quotation marks. If you use this information in your display or project report, you must rewrite it using your own words. Copying is called **plagiarism**; it is dishonest and illegal.

People in your community are another source of information. Earth scientists work as teachers in high schools and colleges. There may be geologists and meteorologists working in an agriculture or conservation office in your county. Airports and television stations may have meteorologists working as "weathermen." There may be astronomers working at a museum or **planetarium**. If you live near an ocean, you may find oceanographers working at research stations nearby. Asking for the help of a professional earth scientist may seem scary, especially if you don't know the person. However, you should not worry about it. Introduce yourself and briefly explain your idea. You will probably be surprised at how friendly and willing the scientist will be.

Earth scientists are usually eager to talk about their work.

CHAPTER 3

Planning Your Project

Once you have decided what earth science problem you want to investigate, the next step is to decide how you will do the investigation. An experimental design describes the materials that are needed and how they will be used. In a scientific investigation, the answers to a problem come from the experiments that are done.

More About Experimental Design

As you learned in Chapter 2, a well-designed experiment is done under **controlled conditions**. One condition, the independent variable, is changed on purpose. A second condition, the dependent variable, is measured as it changes in response to the independent variable. All other conditions must not be allowed to change at all. The cause of any measured change should only be the result of a change in the independent variable.

A well-designed experiment will insure that the data collected are meaningful. Suppose we had only two jars in the acid rain experiment—one with tap water and one with acid. If the difference in mass of the marble chips at the end of two weeks was very small, what would your conclusion be? Is the small difference really due to the acid? Could it be due to something in the marble chips that we didn't notice? What would your conclusion be if the marble chip in tap water lost a little more mass than the one in acid? Results like these are confusing.

One way to help make sure that you know what your data mean is to repeat the experiment. Each repetition is called a **trial**. How many trials are needed depends on the kind of data being collected. Five trials usually produce reliable data, so we used five jars in each group in the acid rain experiment. This allows us to do five trials at the same time. You can always increase the number of trials if you need to.

Another way to improve the chances of knowing what the data mean is by testing a hypothesis in as many ways as possible. The geologist would want to make observations on many different glaciers over long periods of time before accepting the hypothesis about how the ice moves.

If you find an earth scientist to help you, ask that person to check your experimental design. Ask the scientist to look for conditions that need to be controlled. If no scientist is helping you, you must have a responsible adult check your design. Perhaps your teacher or parent can review your plan to at least make sure that it is safe.

Lab Notebook

Everything about a scientific investigation is written in a lab notebook. You will need a spiral-bound notebook or a three-ring binder for your science project. Since loose pieces of paper can get lost, write everything in the lab notebook.

*If you have loose pieces of paper, you can tape them
into your lab notebook.*

The first page should have the project's title and your name. Your teacher or the science fair rules may require that you include additional information on the first page. A table of contents on the next page will help readers find each part of your project.

As you learned in Chapter 2, the first entry in your lab notebook should state the purpose of your investigation. Next, transfer the useful information from your note cards to your lab notebook. Be sure to include all the information about each source. Notes from interviews with scientists should also be in your lab notebook. There should be a complete list of materials and a detailed description of how you will use them. All measurements and observations you make during the experiment need to be neatly recorded in the notebook. Your notebook doesn't have to be perfectly neat, but your handwriting should be clear enough for other people to read. Your notebook will be a part of your science fair display and the judges will look at it.

☞ *Materials*

A list of materials should identify everything that will be needed to do the project. Be sure to state how much of each item will be needed, too. You may wish to put the list in alphabetical order. The example below shows a list of materials for the acid rain experiment.

Materials

balance	plastic jars, 10
graduated cylinder	vinegar (acid), 125 ml
marble chips, 10	water, 375 ml

For some projects, materials may have to be ordered from a supply company. If you need to order something, ask an adult for help. You will need to allow several weeks for delivery of your order. Companies that sell earth science materials are listed at the end of this book.

☞ *Procedure*

A detailed description of each of the steps in the experiment—in the order in which they are done—is the procedure. Your procedure should be written in your lab notebook. It must be approved by an adult, like the scientist you asked to help you.

You may find a **flow chart** useful. It is a simple version of your procedure. It will quickly remind you of the steps and their correct order. The sample flow chart is for the acid rain experiment.

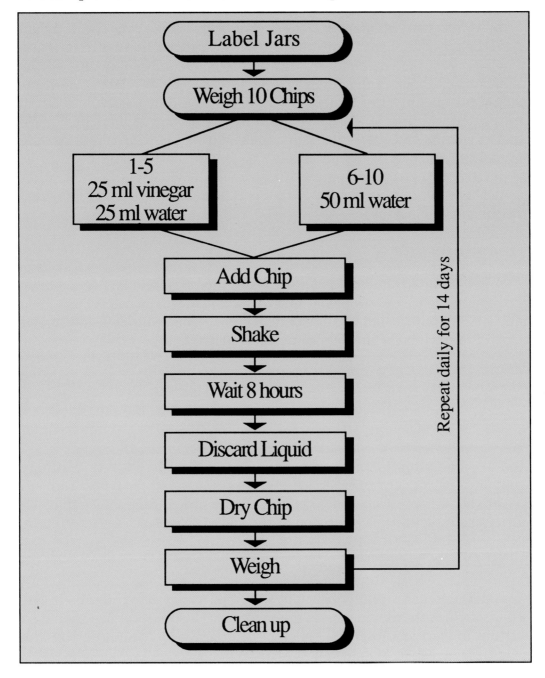

Time Schedule

If you start planning your project several months before it is due, you will have time to enjoy your work. There will be time to correct errors and redesign experiments. You may find yourself doing a whole series of related experiments—and that makes science fun!

You will need time to decide on a topic, do library research, gather materials, plan and conduct the experiment, analyze the data, write a report, and make a display. Estimate how much time each step will take, then add a little more time. Allow plenty of time for the delivery of materials if you must order something.

Sample Time Schedule for an Earth Science Investigation

Week 1:   Choose a problem
Week 2:   Plan the experiment and gather materials
          (This might take more than one week.)
Week 3:   Conduct the first trial of the experiment
Week 4:   Analyze the data; redesign the experiment if needed
Week 5:   Repeat additional trials of the experiment
Week 6:   Finish collecting and analyzing data
Week 7:   Make the display
Week 8:   Practice the oral report; present your project

CHAPTER 4

Doing Your Project

Safety

Safety is always the first concern in every step of designing and doing an earth science project. As described in Chapter 2, one of the first things you should do is find a scientist who will help you. If you don't have the help of a scientist, you must at least have an adult who will review your experiment for possible dangers.

You will need a place where you can work on your project. A table in your classroom or in your own room at home can be used. Maybe someone can help you set up a workbench in your garage, storage room, or basement. When you are selecting the best place for your work, be sure to consider your needs. How much space will be needed to do your experiment? Where will you store your materials when you aren't using them? Will you need water? How will you clean up?

If you use any chemicals, you will need to wear a rubber apron, gloves, and safety goggles. Be careful what you touch while you are using chemicals. Keep your hands away from your face and out of your mouth. Use chemicals only when an adult supervisor is present to help you.

Don't forget! **Always** *use safety equipment.*

If your field study requires that you go out into the woods, find out about poisonous plants in your area. Learn to recognize plants like poison ivy so you can avoid them. Protect yourself by wearing long-sleeved shirts and pants. Ask your supervisor to go with you the first time you collect data in the field.

If your project involves using a boat, learn water safety rules and obey them. *Never* go out in a boat alone. An adult should make every trip with you. If you are studying the shore, wade in water only where you can see the bottom.

If you will need electricity, try to find battery-powered equipment. Keep all cords and wires away from water and chemicals. Remember that electrical equipment can get hot.

Before you actually begin any part of your procedure, you must write a detailed description of what you will do in each step. Have your adult supervisor check your steps for possible hazards. Avoid working alone. Someone should be near enough to hear or see if you should need help.

Keeping a Record of Your Results

After you have designed your experiment—but before you actually begin doing it—you will need to decide how you will record the data. What measurements and observations should you record? There are two kinds of observations. A **qualitative observation** does not use measurements—it uses words to make comparisons. The following statements are qualitative observations:

> The liquid in all jars turned cloudy.
> The marble chips in acid became smoother than those in water.

A **quantitative observation** does use measurements—it uses numbers to make comparisons. The following statements are quantitative observations:

> Marble chip #1 weighed 6.2 grams.
> Marble chip #3 lost 2.8 grams in 14 days.

Quantitative observations are the most precise. They provide more accurate information to use in evaluating the hypothesis. Plan to record as many quantitative observations as possible. You can't write down too much!

☞ *Data Charts*

All observations are written in the lab notebook. Using a **data chart** will make recording observations easier and faster. In a data chart, the independent and dependent variable are identified. The values for the independent variable are filled in before the experiment. The values for the dependent variable are filled in as the experiment proceeds. You can't expect to remember everything you saw and measured during an experiment. The data chart should be ready to use before the experiment begins. A page in the lab notebook for recording data during the acid rain experiment might look like the sample data chart.

Data Chart

Chip Number	Mass (g)																
	Day Number																
	0	1	2	3	4	5	6	7	8	9	10	11	12	13	14	15	16
1																	
2																	
3																	
4																	
5																	
6																	
7																	
8																	
9																	
10																	

Scientists must be **unbiased** when observing what happens in experiments. They record exactly what they see and measure, even if the data do not match their predictions. Remember, with the scientific method you can't get "wrong" results.

When your observations are not what you expected, you look for an explanation. Maybe your hypothesis was not correct. Then you can state a new one that better explains the observations from your experiment. Maybe you found an uncontrolled variable in your experiment. Then you can redesign the experiment and do it again. Whatever the results, you will always learn something of value from an experiment.

☞ *Metric Measurements*

All scientists make measurements using the metric system. No matter what language they speak, they all understand and use the same metric units for length, volume, mass, and temperature. You should use the metric system, too.

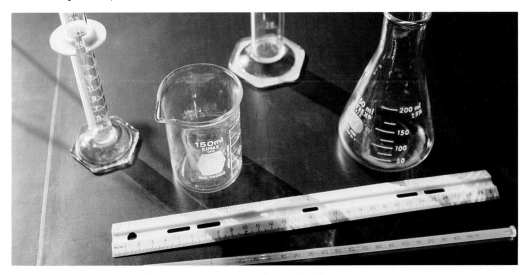

Try to use the metric system for all of your measurements.

A meter stick or metric ruler is used to measure length. A **meter**, the basic metric unit of length, is divided into smaller units called **centimeters** and **millimeters**. Just as 100 cents equal one dollar, 100 centimeters equal one meter. Millimeters are very small—1000 millimeters equal one meter. Select the unit that best measures the variable. You would use centimeters to measure the length of a footprint, but you might use meters for the width of a stream.

Earth scientists use a **graduated cylinder** to measure volume. A graduated cylinder is much like a measuring cup. A **liter**, the basic metric unit of volume, is divided into **milliliters**. One thousand milliliters equals one liter. Unless a larger volume is needed, most materials are measured in milliliters.

A **balance** is a tool used to measure mass. The basic metric unit is the **gram**. A dollar bill has a mass of about one gram. The mass of large objects is measured in **kilograms.**

A thermometer is used to measure temperature. It is marked in degrees Celsius (C) for metric measurement. Water boils at 100°C and freezes at O°C. Body temperature is 37°C and room temperature is about 20°C.

Analyzing Results

Sometimes an experiment yields so much data that it's hard to see what it all means. There are several methods scientists use to help make things easier. First, when an experiment has several trials, an average for the trials can be calculated. For example, suppose you have determined the amount of mass lost in each of the 10 jars in the acid rain experiment. You can find the average mass lost by the experimental group—the chips in jars 1-5. Add together the masses lost by each chip; then, divide the sum by 5 (the number of chips in the experimental group). The answer is the average mass lost. Find the average mass lost by the control group in the same way. Now you can compare the averages.

Data		Calculating an average	
.2 g	.2 g	.44 g	
.4 g	.4 g	5⟌2.20	
.7 g	.7 g	200	The average mass
.5 g	.5 g	20	loss of the chips is
.4 g	.4 g	20	.44 g.
	2.2 g	0	

Second, scientists use graphs to help them see patterns in the data. The graph most frequently used by scientists is a **line graph**. In a line graph there are two axes—one vertical and one horizontal. The **horizontal axis** shows the independent variable. The **vertical axis** shows the dependent variable. Each axis is labelled with the name of the variable, the units used to measure it, and a scale of number values. The graph has a title that tells what observations are being shown. After the data are plotted, the points are connected with a line. In order to compare many sets of data, several lines can be plotted together. Each set is identified by a different color or pattern. The sample below shows a line graph and a data chart used to plot the graph.

Effects of Acid Rain on the Mass of Marble Chips

Day Number	Average Mass (g)	
	Experimental Group	Control Group
0	21.2	20.8
2	21.0	20.8
4	20.5	20.6
6	20.1	20.6
8	19.7	20.5
10	19.2	20.5
12	18.5	20.4
14	17.8	20.3

There are several other types of graphs. They include circle graphs and bar graphs. These types are used to display data. They are not usually useful in analyzing data. More information about these graphs can be found in Chapter 5.

Drawing Conclusions

When all the data have been collected and analyzed, conclusions are drawn. Conclusions tell what the data mean. Do the data support the hypothesis? If they do not, what new hypothesis does the data suggest? What new experiments might better test the hypothesis? What new problems can be identified? Write all your conclusions in your lab notebook. Try to explain all of your conclusions. Go back over the notes in your lab notebook. If you think you made any mistakes, explain how you think these mistakes may have influenced your observations. Remember, there is no such thing as being "wrong," but it's important to explain each conclusion you write.

Another important part of your conclusions is an explanation of how the results of your experiment might be used by other people. For example, if you found that the chips in the jars containing vinegar lose more mass than those in water, you could discuss what acid rain might do to marble monuments and buildings. Science fair judges are very interested in what uses you can think of for your experimental results.

CHAPTER 5

Presenting Your Project

The last step of the scientific method is to tell others about the experiment and its results. Other scientists need to know what work has been done. Scientists can tell about their work in many ways. One way is to write an article for a magazine or a book. Another way is to give a speech at a scientific meeting. When you take part in a science fair, you are telling others about your experiment, too.

Part of a scientist's job is to tell others about their work.

Writing a Report

Most science fair judges expect to see a written report, not just a lab notebook. Some fairs have rules about what to include, as well as their order. Before you begin writing, find out what the local rules are.

Written reports can be typed or printed by computer. If you write neatly, handwriting is fine, too. It's best to put the pages in a folder or a binder.

The first page, called the title page, should have the title of your project and your name. Your teacher might ask you to also write the date, the school's name, and your grade. The second page should be a table of contents to help readers find the parts of your report.

The remaining parts of the written report follow the same organization as the lab notebook. The lab notebook is the resource of all the information in the report. The following list shows what to include and the order:

Contents for Written Report

Purpose	Data
Background Research	Conclusions
Hypothesis	Bibliography
Materials	Acknowledgements
Procedure	

The statement of purpose tells what you wanted to find out in your earth science project. In the background research section, summarize what you learned in the library and from earth scientists and other experts. Your explanations in this section should help the reader understand your hypothesis and experimental design.

A list of materials, the procedure that shows how you used them, and the data and observations you made are in the next sections. You should include any line graphs that you made to help you analyze your data. You may also want to include other types of graphs that display your data. These graphs are described in the next section of this book.

Using your lab notebook as a guide, state your conclusions. Discuss possible errors and describe new problems suggested by your results. Explain how your results can be applied in our world.

A bibliography lists all the sources of information you used in writing your report. The entries are in alphabetical order by the author's last name. Two examples follow to help you write a bibliography:

For a magazine:
Barinaga, Marcia. "The secret of saltiness." Science 254:664-665 (1991).

For a book:
Hodges, Laurent. Environmental pollution. New York:Holt, Rinehart and Winston, 1977.

In the final section, you should thank everyone who helped you with your project. Name each person and tell how that person helped.

Making Graphs to Show Your Data

Earth scientists often need to graph the data collected during an experiment to understand what the data mean. They most often use line graphs. How to make a line graph is explained in Chapter 4. Other types of graphs are used to display data because they pack a lot of information into a small space. They make data easier to understand.

When you want to compare several groups, you can use a **bar graph**. In this kind of graph, bars are drawn to represent the average measured for each group. Bar graphs are a lot like line graphs. The horizontal axis is used to represent the independent variable, and the vertical axis is used to represent the dependent variable.

Drawing a bar graph takes careful planning. The height of each bar must represent the average for one group. You must decide how high the tallest bar should be. All the bars should be the same width. Look at the following data chart and bar graph as an example:

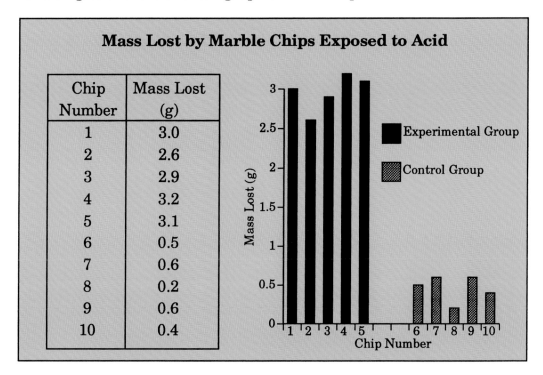

Mass Lost by Marble Chips Exposed to Acid

Chip Number	Mass Lost (g)
1	3.0
2	2.6
3	2.9
4	3.2
5	3.1
6	0.5
7	0.6
8	0.2
9	0.6
10	0.4

A **circle graph** is another way to display information. It is the type of graph to use when you have several parts that make up a whole. For example, in a project on the earth's crust, you might find out what elements make up the rocks of the crust. A large circle represents all of them. The circle is then divided into parts. The size of a slice of the circle represents how much of the total is a particular element. A circle graph is shown below.

Circle Graph

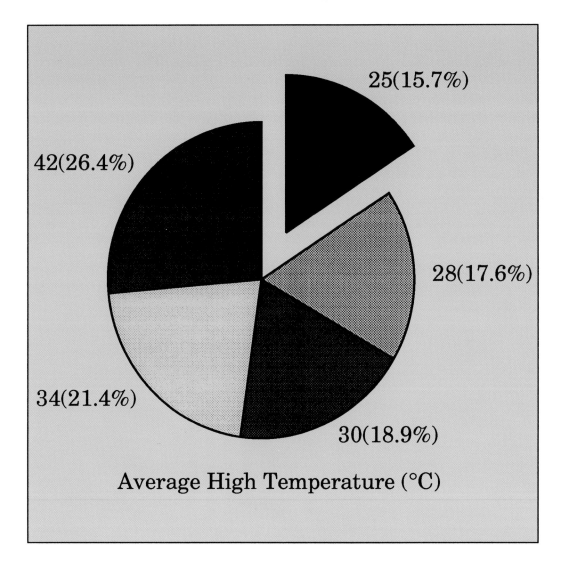

Average High Temperature (°C)

A **pictograph** is constructed like a bar graph, except that it uses a repeating symbol to represent the amount. If there is a fraction in the amount, only a part of the symbol is used. Pick a symbol that fits your project. Take some time to plan a pictograph's layout. Decide how many symbols you will need in each row. You will use many copies of the symbol, and all of them in the pictograph should look the same. You could carefully draw your design and then make many copies on a copy machine. You could also cut out the symbol from a small piece of cardboard and then trace around it to make the rows.

Pictograph

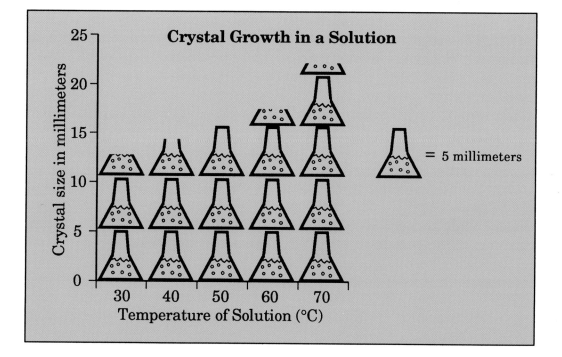

All graphs must be clearly labelled so the reader will know what the numbers mean. Each graph must have a title that tells what information is being shown. Lettering should be neat. You can buy press-on letters at an office supply store. Choose a size that fits the graphs you have planned. You can also trace around a stencil. If you can use a computer, a graphing program will arrange and print the graphs for you. If you make the graphs yourself, you might want to use graph paper. Graph paper has lines printed on it that divide the page into squares. These squares can be used as guidelines in planning a graph. You can buy graph paper at an office or school supply store.

Organizing Your Display

When you visit a science fair, what do you notice first? Usually, a good looking display catches your eye. The lettering is easy to read. The drawings, photos, and graphs are neat and colorful. The display tells a complete story of the project.

The most common display is a three-sided board that stands by itself. It should be large enough but not too large. You can buy cardboard or foam-filled display boards at an office or art supply store. These boards come in different colors and sizes. They are ready to write on, tape on, pin on, or staple on. You can also build a board out of plywood or peg board. These materials make sturdy displays, but they will be heavy. You can even cut up a large cardboard box into a three-sided board for your display. You might want to cover the brown cardboard with white paper or paint. Most science fairs have limited space for each project. Check the rules to see that your board will not be too large. Consider how you will carry your board to class or the science fair before you make your choice, too.

Put your title on the center section of the display. Choose letters that are large and easy to read. You can use two-inch press-on letters, or you can cut out letters of colored art paper. Plan the spacing of the title before you start putting any letters in place. Don't forget to check the spelling, too.

The center section will usually be seen first. So below the title, put some interesting graphs of data, photos, or drawings that show your observations.

On the left side, state the purpose or the hypothesis of your project. Include a brief summary of your experimental design. You might want to use your flow chart instead of a step-by-step procedure. Photographs of you doing your project will add interest and show the judges that you did the experiment yourself.

On the right side, show any data that didn't fit on the center section. Then briefly state your conclusions. If you have room, you can include some ideas for new experiments.

Before you attach any of the pieces, place them on the board to see how they look. Move them around until you find a pleasing, simple layout.

There's always something exciting about a science fair!

Have someone check your printing for correct spelling, punctuation, and grammar. Make sure everything is labelled correctly.

Now you are ready to put the display together. Select a glue that doesn't wrinkle your paper. You can also use double-stick tape on the back of the paper. Try to avoid using staples.

Stand your display up and see how it looks. Place your written report and lab notebook on the table in front of the display. The rest of the table

Try to make your display as interesting as possible.

space can also be used. You can put out samples of the materials you used or the products of your experiment. If you do put objects on the table, be sure they do not cover up the lower part of your display board.

Talking to the Judges or to Your Class

You will probably be expected to talk about your project to science fair judges or to your class. In four or five minutes you will have to do the following:

★   Introduce yourself.

★   Give the title of your project.

★   State the purpose of your project.

★   Tell why you chose this project.

★   Explain what you did.

★   Show your results.

★   Explain what you learned.

★   State your conclusions.

★   Ask if there are any questions.

You can use notes to help you remember what you want to say. Plan your speech and then practice it in front of other people. Ask your practice audience for helpful ideas. After practicing several times, put away your notes. Try using just your display to help you remember what you want to say. If you still feel better with notes, use them. However, try not to just read from them.

When you are talking to the judges or to your class, stand to the side of your display. Point out the parts as you talk about them. Use your written report to show details to the judges. Talk slowly so you can think about what you are saying. If you get nervous or confused, take a deep breath. Pause. Then go on with your explanation.

When you are finished, ask your listeners if they have any questions. If you don't know the answer, just say you don't know. If you don't understand a question, ask the person to repeat or rephrase it. Before you answer, you might want to state the question yourself. Then the judge, or a listener, will know you heard the question correctly.

Don't be afraid of the judges. They enjoy talking to young scientists.

Judging of Your Project

The science fair judges who visit you at your display will check your project for an award. Each science fair usually has its own judging sheets. However, the following areas are used most often:

★ Scientific thought—The judges will check to see if your project follows the scientific method. They will look for a clearly stated problem and proper procedure, including the use of controls. They will check that the conclusions are supported by the results. The judges will look for evidence that you did your own experiment.

★ Creative ability—The judges will want to know how you got your idea. This is the score that will be low if you did only an exhibit or demonstration, or if someone else did the actual work. If your idea came from a book like this one, explain how you used your imagination to develop the project. More points will usually be given for scientific thought and creative ability than for the other areas.

★ Understanding—Your display should show what you learned. Judges will ask questions to see if you understand the key scientific ideas in your project. They will want to know what background sources you read, and if you prepared a bibliography. They will look at your display and written report to see if they tell the complete story and give answers to questions about the topic.

★ Clarity—The judges will score projects higher if you clearly state the problem, experimental design, data, and conclusions. Writing should be easy to read and understand, even for the average person.

★ Technical skill—The judges will try to decide if you had the knowledge and skill to do the experiment and make the measurements yourself. They will want to know if anyone helped you and how. They will look at graphs in your written report and on your display to see if they are done correctly. Finally, judges check to see that you put thought and effort into the building of your display.

Final Words of Encouragement

Doing a science fair project takes time and hard work. When you finish your project, take pride in what you have done. You have not just been "acting" like a scientist—you have been a scientist. You used the scientific method to investigate an earth science problem. You now know how to ask a question and find out the answer. Maybe you even discovered the excitement and wonder of doing science.

Where do you go from here? Maybe you'll want to start another project for next year's science fair. Let your imagination lead the way!

All of your hard work will be worth it!

Companies That Sell Scientific Supplies

Carolina Biological Supply Co.
2700 York Road
Burlington, NC 27215
1-800-334-5551 (East of the Rockies)
1-800-547-1733 (Rockies and West)
1-800-632-1231 (North Carolina)

Connecticut Valley Biological
Supply Co., Inc.
P.O. Box 326
Southampton, MA 01073
1-800-628-7748 (U.S.)
1-800-282-7757 (Mass.)

Edmund Scientific Co. (colored filters)
101 E. Gloucester Pike
Barrington, NH 08007-1380
1-609-573-6250

Nasco
P.O. Box 901
Fort Atkinson, WI 53538-0901
1-800-558-9595

Ward's
P.O. Box 92912
Rochester, NY 14692-9012
1-800-962-2660

GLOSSARY

astronomy - study of objects seen in the sky.

balance - a tool used to measure mass.

conclusions - what you interpret the results of an experiment to mean.

control group - a group in an experiment in which as many variables as possible are kept constant because they could affect the outcome of the experiment.

controlled conditions - making sure that anything that changes during an experiment is done on purpose.

data - the observations and measurements that you make in an experiment.

dependent variable - the factor or condition that changes as a result of the presence of, or a deliberate change you make in, the independent variable.

ellipse - elongated circle or oval.

experimental design - the plans you make so you can do an experiment. The design includes what you will use and how you intend to use them.

experimental group - a group in which all variables are the same as those in the control group *except* for the factor that you are following in your experiment.

flow chart - a list that writes out a shortened version of the steps you want to follow in doing your experiment. As you complete each step, you should check it off the list.

geologist - scientist who studies the history of earth recorded in rocks.

graduated cylinder - a tool used to measure the volume of a liquid.

hypothesis - a statement that gives a possible answer to a question, sometimes called an "educated guess." To see if it is true or not, a hypothesis is tested by doing an experiment.

horizontal axis - the line at the bottom of a graph that represents the independent variable.

independent variable - the factor or condition that you want to study. In an experiment, you intentionally change this factor.

mass - the amount of matter, or "stuff," that is present. Weight is often confused with mass. Weight is the pulling force of gravity on matter.

meteorology - study of air and weather.

oceanographer - scientist who studies the ocean.

paleontologist - scientist who studies ancient life using fossils.

plagiarism - copying word-for-word what someone else has written and not giving credit to that person.

planetarium - room in which a model sky can be projected on the ceiling.

prediction - what you think will happen in an experiment.

qualitative observation - an outcome of an experiment that is not an amount that can be measured, such as color.

quantitative observation - an outcome of an experiment that is measurable, such as numbers of individuals.

scientific method - a systematic strategy scientists use to discover answers to questions about the world. It includes making a hypothesis, testing the hypothesis with experiments, collecting and analyzing the results, and arriving at a conclusion.

talus - rock at the base of a cliff.

trial - a test that is one of a group of repeated tests.

tsunami - sea wave produced by an underwater earthquake.

unbiased - not allowing your preferences to interfere with collecting or analyzing data in an experiment.

variable - some factor in an experiment that can be changed.

vertical axis - the line on the left side of a graph that represents the dependent variable.

INDEX

Astronomy 11
Average, calculating 30

Bibliography, making 34

Conclusions, coming to 9, 32

Data 8
Data charts 28
Display 38-40
    construction 38
    lettering 38

Earth Science 10-11
Experimental design 7, 21-22
    variables 12
    controls 8, 12,21

Flow chart 24

Geology 11
Graphs, types of 31, 35-38
    bar graph 35
    circle graph 36
    line graph 31
    pictograph 37

Hypothesis 5

Judging 41-43
    talking to judges 41
    scoring of project 42-43

Lab notebook 18, 22-23

Library, information in 18-19
    card or on-line catalog 18
    Reader's Guide to Periodical
    Literature 18

Mass 8
Materials 23, 45
Meteorology 11
Metric system 29-30
Models 16-17

Notes, taking 19

Observations 4, 27-28

Procedure 23-24
Projects, types of 10-17
    demonstrations 11-12
    exhibits 11
    investigations 12-17
Purpose of investigation 18

Record keeping 27-28
Report, written 33-35
Resource people 20
Results, analyzing 30-31

Safety 26-27
Scientific method 4-9

Time schedule 25
Trial 21

Weathering 6